one
and done

Austin

lake langley

Print ISBN: 978-1-66787-738-9

eBook ISBN: 978-1-66787-739-6

Printed in the United States of America

table of contents

introduction

They, whoever *they* are, say that in order to write well, you should write about what you know.

I have been single almost my entire adult life … and I'm now in my fifties. I've dated here and there and have been married twice, with an eighteen-year-span between marriages. My first marriage lasted two-and-a-half years; the second, a whopping eight months. It's not that I can't commit. I love being in a committed relationship. I just, according to my therapist, don't do well when someone attaches their wagon to mine. He might be right. Maybe I do have a small commitment issue.

So, getting back to what I know: One-night stands.

And I've had a few.

Not the life I envisioned for myself. My plan since I was sixteen was to marry the man of my dreams shortly after high school. We'd have four kids, I'd be a stay-at-home mommy, live in a nice big house, drive a big-ass suburban, and live happily ever after with my amazing husband who adored me.

Unfortunately, "the best laid plans … o' mice an' men gang aft agley." (Robert Burns)

Gang aft agley basically means, get fucked up.

I couldn't have said it any better.

I have also never been one for following rules set for boys versus rules for girls. In fact, I firmly believe I was a man in several of my past lives and must have been a real asshole, because I've dealt with plenty in this lifetime. I have also been put in my place with regard to being a girl but have come out kicking and screaming every time. To some, I may seem a bit loud and perhaps even slutty. That's okay. This book will prove I have a voice and have been a bit *adventurous at times*, but no more than most guys I know.

The series you're about to embark on are memoirs of some of my most favorite encounters. My *Best Of*, if you will.

And if you're wondering why I'm writing this under a pseudonym? One reason should be obvious: this is a book about a subject some people can't even talk about above a whisper.

Reasons two through one hundred: I have kids and grandkids, although I have a feeling my grandkids will be supportive of my sexcapades the way I would have been supportive of my grandmother's ... all too happy to hear their grandma is gettin' some! My boys, however, will pray for hot pokers to burn their eyes out of their sockets and to be stabbed in their ears until they bleed should the contents of this book be brought to their knowledge.

So, as in the cases of Mark Twain and George Henry, I pray that, should my identity be brought to light, you forget it just as easily as you found it. Plus, as much as I hope this book makes it into the hands of as many of you as possible, I don't think this book will be what catapults me into the world of the rich and famous. Okay, I'll take rich, happy to leave the famous.

All of that said, should you be one of the lucky ones, the ones who are married but may go through challenging experiences, wondering if it's worth it to stay, please know the grass may look greener on my side, and sometimes it is. But as much as my married girlfriends claim to live vicariously through me now and again, women like me live vicariously through women like you, too.

I dedicate this book to you, the reader. I hope you enjoy it. I hope it makes you laugh. And I hope it gets you excited to spend some time with Bob (your battery-operated boyfriend) or, if you're lucky enough, the real man in your life. I hope it helps you realize you're not alone in this world of things that are taboo due to religion or gender. Most of all, I hope this book sparks a memory of your own past loves and life experiences. Enjoy.

Side note … all stunts in this book were performed by a consenting professional and, at times, without safety gear. Please do not attempt at home … or abroad.

Disclaimer … in this world of sue-happy individuals, I would like to state that although some of the characters in my book are based on real people, all the names have been changed, as well as some of the locations. If anyone believes themselves to be one of the characters in my story, don't. I have compiled stories from different experiences and encounters, creating collages from true stories and rolling them into one. These are my memories, the way *I* remember them, adlibbing where needed. It is a story, after all.

one and done

Austin, Texas
Fall 2008

chapter 1

"Hello?" I whispered groggily, finally realizing it was my phone ringing and not my alarm. My voice, not surprisingly, sounded like it belonged to a chain smoker.

"Lake? Did I wake you?" Ava didn't sound apologetic at all.

I pulled my phone away from my ear, checking the time, *6:18 a.m. Looks like I slept through my 5:30 alarm.* I love waking up early to the sun at 5:30 a.m. in the summer. But this was late September, and the light creeping through the east-facing window was minimal. "Ugh, seriously," I griped, "late sunrises kill me. Are you on your way to work?" I asked, now surprised at sounding like the Albino from *Princess Bride*.

Ava laughed. "Late sunrises? Oh Booboo, you and your 'rise with the sun' cracks me up!"

"Hey, it worked for sweet Tommy." I yawned while wiping the sleep from my eyes.

"Tommy?"

"Tommy? Thomas Jefferson! Duh!" I love quirky human traits and felt a small, intimate connection with the third President of the United States, whom I read loved the same.

"Oh, booboo, so scholarly of you," Ava said, her tone mimicking that of an aristocrat. I could picture her squinting her eyes and pursing her lips as she spoke.

I pursed my lips to match what I envisioned hers to be and echoed back, "*Mmm*, you know me."

Since moving to Austin, Ava (whom I met ten years earlier through a mutual friend) and I had become even closer than when she lived near me in Denver, Colorado. She didn't know many people in Austin, and I was the only one of her friends in Denver awake (most of the time) during her drive to work with the one-hour time difference.

"What's up?" I asked, slowly pushing myself up.

"So, I was thinking. Any chance you're up for a visit?"

Led by the aroma of coffee pre-set on a timer the previous night, I strolled out of my bedroom and into the kitchen. Since the sun wasn't available to wake me during what I call my hibernation period, the smell of coffee usually did. "Yeah, I mean, I don't see why not? What's a good weekend for you?" I asked, as I poured myself a large cup of coffee, complete with creamer. As I listened to Ava rattle off her availability, I retrieved my appointment book from my handbag, penciling in the dates she gave me. All I needed now was to check with my sister to see if she was open to watch my thirteen-year-old son, (whose sperm donor of a father was MIA and had been going on almost four years now). If my sister was available, I'd be in Austin the last weekend of October, just three short weeks away.

* * *

Austin, Texas
October 31, 2008

As I landed in Austin, I flipped my phone open and pressed the green telephone symbol to turn it on. I watched for the four bars at the right-hand corner to show I had service and then texted Ava the minute I walked onto the jetway. She called back immediately.

"Hello?" I whispered quietly as to not annoy the passengers in front of or behind me.

"You're here? You're early!" She said, sounding excited and surprised.

"Yeah, but it'll probably take me a good twenty or thirty minutes to make it to the pickup area, right?" This was my first time in Austin, so I had no idea what to expect.

"Uh, no," Ava deadpanned. "Austin may be the capital of Texas, but the airport is super small. You're going to get off the plane, walk about three minutes, go down the escalator toward baggage claim, and then straight out the doors. I'm running," Ava paused a second, "on time, actually, but you weren't supposed to be here for another twenty minutes. Sorry, Boo!"

"No worries, Angel face. I'll wait for you outside and soak up some much-needed humidity." Closing my phone, I followed my fellow passengers toward baggage claim. True to Ava's word, I walked about twenty-five yards to the escalators, rode them down, and, since I didn't check a bag, walked straight outside. All of which took me a whopping ten minutes.

The air here felt heavy compared to the oxygen-deprived, arid city I had left just hours earlier. I love humidity, absolutely love it, and am in awe at how beautifully it transforms my skin from looking like a shriveled-up raisin to a nice, plump grape. I found a large flowerpot and leaned against it as I waited for Ava, instantly jealous of her for moving here. It was 5:30 and still light outside. If I were home in Colorado, the sun would be bidding me adieu as it set behind the Rocky Mountains. From my flowerpot, I marveled at how aesthetically pleasing everything was. Palm trees and flowers in purple, yellow, pink, and red seemed to be everywhere I looked, smothered against a backdrop of green foliage. I know comparison is the thief of all joy, yet I couldn't help but compare it to the barren, exhaust-filled pickup area at Denver International Airport.

I closed my eyes and breathed in the thick air as I listened to my surroundings. Birds chirped as they took flight, carrying their song with them from one location to the next, mixed with the sound of a polite horn

9

tap here and there as drivers signaled others to either pull in front of them or alert them, they were about to get hit. It's anyone's guess when your eyes are closed. My phone vibrated, startling me away from my assumptions. Ava's name was on the screen, and I quickly flipped it open. "Yo!" I answered.

"Where are you? I'm almost there."

I abandoned my flowerpot and walked to the right of the huge concrete pillar in front of me, "I'm at four. That's what the pillar says."

"Oh, okay, okay, you're toward the middle."

Ava and I continued to chat until I saw her car. "I see you!" I waved, snapping my phone shut. Ava pulled right to me, threw her Tahoe in park, and hurried out.

"Well, hi, Boo!" she said, giving me a quick hug (Ava's not a big hugger), then opened the back hatch and grabbed my small duffle bag. "This is all you brought?"

"That's it," I answered. "I travel light these days!"

Ava's face transformed into sexy sophistication as she raised her eyebrows and slowly blinked. "Impressive," she drawled, her lips exaggerating a pout.

"God, it's good to see you." I said, realizing just how much I had missed her and her many facial expressions. She tossed my bag inside and I watched as all five-foot-nothing of her grabbed the hatch strap, pulled it toward her, and slammed the back shut. She reminded me of a contestant on *The Price Is Right* as they reach up to spin the Big Wheel. I couldn't help but marvel at her petite ways.

As I climbed into the passenger side, Ava asked if I was hungry, and, of course, I was! (Side note. I'm almost *always* hungry.) "I'm starving, and I am dying for a Whataburger!"

"You know Austin is known for its food, right?" Ava contorted her expression, seemingly appalled, then continued, "We have so many amazing restaurants and food trucks and you want Whataburger?"

I looked back at her, reflecting the same appalled look she was giving me. "You know we don't have Whataburger in Colorado, right?"

Ava rolled her eyes as if in disgust. "Okay, Whataburger it is." And with that, she made a hard right turn.

Minutes later, I was devouring the burger of my dreams.

"How do you do that?"

"Do what?" I asked defensively, a mouth full of Whataburger muffling my question.

"Take something I find absolutely disgusting and turn it into something I want to eat? You definitely enjoy your food!" My mouth was so full I had to tilt my head back as to not lose any of the precious burger that was occupying every corner of my mouth.

"It's a gift!"

* * *

With one of the things on my to-do-in-Austin list, checked off, we headed to Ava's apartment on Congress. Ava talked the entire drive, pointing out places of interest and giving me the rundown of what we'd be doing that night and the players involved.

It was Halloween, so I made sure to pack a costume. But instead of dressing up like a slutty nurse, slutty vampire, or slutty cheerleader, I just planned to dress slutty. I'm kidding! Ava and I dressed the same as we would for any Friday night out. I was colorful as usual, wearing a baby-blue Chinese silk cheongsam dress I had happened upon the previous summer. My youngest (of two boys) son and I were in San Francisco for the Centurion Alcatraz open-water swim that I was competing in. After the race, I had my heart set on Chinese food, so the two of us rode the trolley into Chinatown. Dim sum wasn't the only thing I scored. The dress's material was stunning, displaying a raised flower print, its edges delicately embroidered with white and dark blue piping. Sleeveless, it showed off my swimmer's arms, one of my favorite assets. It fell mid-thigh, accentuating my long legs. At only five-foot-seven, my legs account for most of my body. The dress was amazing. Sam Edelman four-inch nude stiletto sandals completed my look. Having treated myself to a blowout before leaving Denver, my beige/blonde, shoulder-length lob was silky smooth, even in this humidity. And since we were going out, I opted for my usual out-on-the-town makeup: mascara, soft light brown eyeliner, and my staple C.O. Bigelow Peppermint lip gloss. And Ava? Ava is always, has always, and will always be a total class act, dressing in her usual: black! Black bell flare slacks, a black satin spaghetti-strap camisole, and black four-inch stiletto heels, all Chanel-accented with gold jewelry. That's how she rolls, and she is stunning. Ava Augustino is Italian-American and looks every bit of it, especially with her dark brown hair combed tightly back in a timeless bun. And she is always tan. Blessed with beautiful olive skin that doesn't seem to age, the sun is her tanner of choice. Other than wearing a soft pinkish lipstick, I don't know that she wore much more makeup than I did. That night, when Ava's new friends asked why we weren't in costume, I informed them we were. I was a cougar (at the ripe age of forty-one) and Ava, six years younger, was a cougar-in-training. *Wrah wrah.*

All dressed up with some place to go, my cub and I started Lake's Big Austin Adventures. First stop: Key Bar on 6th Street, the place to see and be seen, or so I was told. Key Bar is an indoor/outdoor bar that I would describe as rustic and chic. Garage doors lined the entire front of the building. Rolled open, they integrated the inside of the bar with the outdoors and reminded me of old service stations my friends' parents took their cars to when I was young. The air here, however, did not smell of a 1970s oil and grease service station. It smelled of Justin Timberlake's *Rock Your Body* lyrics … *the air is thick, it's smellin' right. Ahhh,* the smell of humidity mixed with a new town. Yum.

On the wall behind the bar, keys of every shape and size were displayed on hooks. There ya go, Key Bar. Sometimes I'm overly impressed at how quickly I figure things out. This bar was definitely cool, and I loved its energetic vibe. After arriving via cab, Ava and I planted our buns on retro metal bar stools. I couldn't decide if they were beat up from use or had been made to look that way. They were clean, and that's all that mattered.

"Hi ladies. What are we drinking tonight?" an adorable bartender asked. He was college age-ish with short dirty-blonde hair, light brown eyes, and a slight scruff that accented his chiseled jawline. With the slightest movement of his mouth, a dimple teased on his left cheek. He was dressed in jeans, a light-gray cotton-blend button down, and a dark gray tie. I wondered if he had come by this trendy style on his own or, did he have a sister or girlfriend who helped with …

"Do you want to stay with the same thing we had at my place?" Ava asked, interrupting my contemplation of our bartender's wardrobe. Redirecting my line of thought to alcohol and knowing firsthand the damage that mixing liquors can do, I answered in the affirmative. "What's your name?" Ava asked our cute bartender.

"Levi," he said smiling, his dimple growing more prominent.

"Okay, Levi. I love your name, by the way." Levi's smile grew, but he pursed his lips, trying to hide what seemed to be embarrassment. "We'll have two tall, not double tall, grape vodka and sodas please!" Levi repeated our order back to us. No sooner had he turned to make our cocktails when I heard Ava's name being squealed from behind us. Ava twirled around and hopped down from the stool to greet a mixed herd of five ladies and gents walking our way. She gave the girl closest to her a quick side hug and back pat. "Savannah, this is my girlfriend Lake that I told you about, from Denver. Lake, this is Savannah." There in front of me stood a cute little early thirty-something with curly, shoulder-length white-blonde hair, bright blue eyes, and a big toothy smile. By the simplicity of her outfit, dressing up for Halloween wasn't her gig, either.

"Lake!" Savannah shrieked, startling me. She opened her arms wide before giving me what I would call a beauty pageant hug, close enough that our faces went over each other's shoulders, but far enough away so as not to mess with her Texas hair. "I've heard so much about you! How are you liking Austin so far?" This question was asked with a very southern drawl. I had been noticing all afternoon that people in Austin don't sound as *Texas* as, say, people from Fort Worth. Don't get me wrong, there was an accent, but it was far softer and not as thick.

"I like it a lot so far. Love the weather!" I said, looking at the large thermometer behind the bar, whose red arrow pointed to seventy degrees.

Dryly, Ava chimed in, "Yeah, what is it in Colorado right now? Forty degrees?" Ava had zero regrets about leaving Denver. Cold weather is not her thing.

"It's not that bad!" I joked. "I would say it was at *least* forty-five when my flight left this afternoon!"

"Uh, *exactly.*"

"So, ya'll see any hotties yet?" Savannah inquired, ignoring our banter as she surveyed the room.

"Excluding our bartender? Not a one!" Ava exclaimed. Now back on her stool, Ava leaned back and looked past me to the far end of the bar. "It's kind of dead tonight."

As Ava and Savannah talked about the deadness of the night, I looked over Savannah's entourage. They seemed to be a good mix of early thirty-something boys and girls. None of whom looked the least bit appetizing. I guess if you're going out on the prowl, the last thing you bring is competition.

"Well, let's have a couple drinks and see how the night progresses. Is this the first place ya'll have been?" Savannah asked.

"Besides taking her to Whataburger? Yes!"

"I do love me a good Texas Whataburger!" I confessed.

"Oh Lake! Isn't it the best?" Savannah said, enthusiastically clasping her hands together. I decided that Savannah reminded me of a 1970's, Miss USA contestant answering questions posed to her by Bob Barker. If she would just say; "And world peace Bob." My night would be complete.

* * *

Two more grape vodka and sodas in, I gave Ava the look that says, *I'm toast and ready to go.* Ava met my look with a yawn, and we laughed at how in sync we were. So different was life now than it had been five years ago when we'd shut the bars down, often desperate to find a cab and head back to her place in Wash Park. Not yet ready for the night to end, we'd make breakfast burritos, down more cocktails, and compare notes about the shenanigans of the night.

Ava, holding a fake pen, mimicked her signature in the air to Levi, gesturing for him to bring us our check.

"Ya'll wanna go to Molotov's?" Savannah asked, emerging from her group.

"All I want to do right now is grab a breakfast burrito off the street, go home, and play some scrabble." Ava droned.

I was totally on board and lifted my almost empty glass to hers. "Cheers to that."

"Please, please, please come with us! Just for one drink?" Savannah begged, her hands together as if in prayer.

Ava and I looked at each other, shrugged, and, tilting our heads slightly to the side, gave our token, *Okay, one drink,* answer.

Closing out the check, Ava turned to me, deflated. Her shoulders were down, and her mouth was drawn like she had failed at something.

"I'm sorry. I don't get it. Usually, there are men everywhere, and I'm talking hot men! I really wanted you to see what Austin had to offer."

"That's not why I came here, Ava." I said. Biting the end of my straw, I sucked the last bit of grape vodka and soda from my glass, "I'm here to see you. Period. What good would it do me to meet a guy from Austin?"

"True." Perking up, Ava continued, "You'll like Molotov's. We'll grab one drink and head home."

"Perf!" I said, swiveling myself away from the bar and in the direction of the many available exits. "*Lesss gooo!*"

chapter 2

Leaving Key Bar, the seven of us walked two short blocks to Molotov's. When we entered, a rush of cold air hit me like I was walking into a meat locker. Outside, the temperature was perfect; the temperature in here … was not. One thing I'm not a fan of is needing a Mr. Rogers-style cardigan indoors when it's warm outside. I rubbed the sides of my arms and glanced around at the hodgepodge of décor as I adjusted to the frigid air. It was Wild West Saloon meets present-day industrial and everything in-between. To my right, a dark, heavy, wooden bar extended from the door and continued about fifteen yards (I'm a swimmer, measuring things by yards makes sense for me) where it met the wall at the far end. I half expected to see Wyatt Earp standing there and, this being Halloween, I'm pretty sure I did … except that this Wyatt Earp was wearing his cowboy hat in front of his manhood, complete with chaps, cowboy boots, and what looked to be nothing else. Despite Katy Perry's "I Kissed a Girl" playing overhead, the song playing in my head was *Do your balls hang low? Do they wobble to and fro? Can you tie 'em in a knot, can you tie 'em in a bow?* I couldn't decide if I was curious enough to see what was covering his backside, if anything at all.

Realizing I was staring at his cowboy hat, I forced my attention to the opposite side of the bar. There was a room divider, something mid-century modernish with brushed gold poles spaced twelve inches apart. Between each pole, three gold chains dangled from the ceiling; jewels of every color were scattered throughout the strands in no particular order. On the other side of this divider was another room. From what I could see, there was a long bar-height table with plumbing pipes for legs. Bar stools lined both sides of the table. Staying with the industrial theme, the stool backs were metal, and the seats were light-colored wood, also with plumbing pipe legs. I stretched my neck and saw several empty tables and chairs throughout the space. The only consistency in the entire space was the dark hardwood floor. It was well cared for, not dull or worn, and made me wonder if they had recently refinished it, which would explain the hint of polyurethane in the air. "Are we staying with the same thing?" Ava asked, interrupting my fascination with all that conflicted in this place aesthetically, yet, which taken as a whole, seemed to work perfectly.

"Sure," I shrugged. It was only one more drink, and I doubted switching liquors would matter at this point.

"Josh said we should get our drinks here because it's less crowded. Once everyone has their cocktails, we'll head upstairs to the rooftop bar," Ava said. From what I had witnessed so far, Josh seemed to be Savannah's main sidekick.

"There's an upstairs?" I asked, but before Ava could answer, Savannah appeared, holding three drinks in her hands. Carefully, I took the one she was barely gripping with her index and middle fingers. "Thank you!" I said, retrieving a handful of bar naps. I wrapped one around my glass that was already sweating and handed out the rest.

"Okay, ya'll, I need a photo!" Savannah exclaimed, setting her drink on the bar that had but a handful of people around it, excluding her entourage. The first photo we took was of me, Ava, and Savannah. Truth be told, it was adorable, a "keeper," if you will. Photo approved, I moved out of the limelight and took Savannah's phone from one of her friends, embracing my new position as photographer.

Pictures out of the way, Ava and I followed Savannah into the next room where I saw a wide wooden staircase that led to the rooftop bar. As we ascended the stairs, the chill of air-conditioning disappeared, and my body began to thaw. I still couldn't believe it was seventy degrees outside, and on Halloween night.

Reaching the top stair, Ava and I continued to follow Savannah's lemmings through the crowded rooftop patio. Rihanna's electro pop "Disturbia" pounded through speakers, vibrating the deck beneath our feet. While training for my first open-water ocean swim from Alcatraz to Aquatic Park the prior July, this song repeated often on my workout playlist. Believing I had missed my calling as a performer (my inability to carry a tune dashed that dream), I lip-synced with Rihanna until the group stopped some distance opposite the staircase. Settling into a loose circle, I glanced around at my new surroundings as Ava engaged in conversation with Savannah. As a lover of architecture and design (Frank Lloyd Wright makes me tingle, and seeing a Home Depot excites me to the point of having to pee), I found this place quite stimulating. Overhead, hundreds of twinkle lights seemed suspended in midair, creating a false ceiling, softly illuminating all that they touched beneath the night sky. More mystical lights circled the trunks of potted palms in large wooden planters, six in total, scattered across the rooftop. Some of the palms (my most favorite tree in the whole wide world) extended beyond the twinkle lights and into the pitch-black night sky while others were short and fat, reminding me of pineapples. Flowers of black, purple, and tangerine skirted their bases. *I wonder if they're fragrant,* I pondered. But it hardly mattered as the scent of propane and fire competed with the aromatic bouquet of men's and women's colognes drifting by on a faint breeze. My gaze shifted from the palms to the groups of people that were sitting on bright orange cushions that softened the hardness of the black-walnut wooden couches and chairs they adorned. Rectangular concrete fire pits sat center stage, where the glow of the flames cast shadows of light and dark on the faces looking toward them. Orange seemed to be the accent color of choice, from the cushions and throw pillows to the glass Chihuly-ish looking pendant lights above the bar. Orange, my favorite color.

Enmeshed with my surroundings, I was caught off guard by a ridiculously attractive man staring at me from across the patio. Our eyes locked. *"Can I buy you a drink?"* he mouthed.

"No," I mouthed back holding up my glass, which was still full. *"I'm good. Thank you."* I smiled my smile, which I've been told resembles Cameron Diaz's, and turned to Ava, looking all wild-eyed. "This guy across the bar asked me if he could buy me a drink and he is Trainer Bob hot!" Ava loves the who-would-play-him-in-a-movie game. Every time I meet a new someone, she begs this question. Ava was also aware I was in love with Bob Harper from the television show *Biggest Loser*. So infatuated was I that when my youngest son came to me one day to inform me that Trainer Bob was gay, my heart broke a tiny bit. I buried my head in the sand and told him to never speak of his future stepfather that way.

"Where is he?" she asked, standing taller and looking over my shoulder. I looked back to where he had been standing and *poof*, he was nowhere to be found.

"He was right over there by the bar," I said, frowning. Just then I heard a "Hi!" over my left shoulder and turned toward it. "Ha! He's right here!" I exclaimed, directing my hand toward him like I was a *Price Is Right* model. There before me stood a delicious specimen of a man. He was tall, I'm guessing six-foot-two since I'm five-foot seven (five-foot-nine or eleven with heels) and he was still a good two to three inches taller than me. At first glance, he appeared to have a great body, at least from what I could tell through his nicely ironed (guessing *dry-clean* ironed) white button-down dress shirt with its sleeves rolled up a quarter of the way, and simple light blue jeans. Mr. Harper's twin had a full head of thick, dark auburn-ish, short-ish, wavy hair and dark eyes, *Dark blue, maybe?* He also had a gorgeous smile that he flashed at us in response to my *Price Is Right* showcasing, complete with a sexy, strong jawline. Admittedly, it was lust at first sight.

"I'm Brad," he said, introducing himself. He moved closer to me, holding out his right hand for me to shake. I looked down at his manly hand and placed my delicate girly hand inside. The feel of his hand was warm as it encased mine, bringing my attention to just how small my hand was compared to his. *Protective hands,* I thought, biting my lip to hide my smile. Keeping my hand in his, he leaned closer to me, his mouth next to my ear he asked, "Do you live close to here?" My insides plummeted with excitement as the warmth of his breath tickled my ear. I pulled away slightly so I could look at him and stare into his dark *blue* eyes.

"Nice to meet you, Brad. I'm Lake. And no," I shook my head as my smile broadened, "I don't live close at all," I answered, my voice straining to be heard over the music. Knowing that if I kept this volume, I'd be hoarse in no time, I leaned into him as he'd done to me, catching a whiff of his cologne. Something woodsy, reminding me of the Black Suede Voluspa candles I had back home. I tip-toed up to his ear, smelling him, wanting to live in the crevice of his neck, "I'm in from Denver," I continued, at a lower volume. "And you?" I asked, looking back into his eyes, our hands never leaving each other's. "Are you from here?"

Brad leaned his face closer to mine, kind of being funny; he stared into my eyes and replied with a wink, "I am."

Reluctantly, I let go of his hand and introduced him to Ava and Savannah. In return, he introduced us to his friend Greg. *Hmmm, he has a friend. I didn't notice.* Greg. He wasn't unattractive, but looking him over, I wouldn't go so far as to say he was attractive either, which meant he was a no-go for Ava.

With the introductions out of the way, Brad asked what brought me to Austin. "Uh, that would be me," Ava offered.

"Ah, so you live here?" Brad said, engaging with her. As they chatted, I watched and listened. Brad's voice was deep, smooth, and soothing, cascading over me like I had teased my finger in a chocolate fountain, allowing the chocolate to drip silkily across my skin. His voice could make a girl wet just from listening. This I learned firsthand. Hotter still was the way he interacted with Ava. He listened to what she was saying and responded accordingly. So many people ask a question without caring to hear the response, seemingly too concerned about their own next comment. He was growing sexier and sexier by the second.

"Has anyone ever told you, you look like Michelle Pfeiffer?" he asked, turning his attention back to me. Can you say … puddle? I was a flipping puddle of goo just from him paying attention to me. *Betcha he's in sales.*

"As a matter of fact." I nodded. "Ever since my junior year of high school when she was in *Grease 2*."

"*Grease 2*? I didn't know there was a sequel to the original *Grease*. So, what do you think of Austin so far?" he asked, changing the subject.

"I really like it here," I said, looking around. *Don't get me wrong, Denver can be equally chic, but it ain't this nice outside in October, that's for damn sure!* "Honestly, what's not to love?"

"Well, good. I'm glad you like it here. I love it, too." Brad said. He looked down at my now almost-empty glass, and continued, "So, Lake? As in Lake Austin? Can I buy you a drink now?"

"Yes, as in, and yes please."

"My tab is open downstairs," he said, nodding toward the staircase. We turned and Brad offered me his left arm, which I gladly accepted. I love holding onto a man this way; it makes me feel connected, like I'm his, even if I'm not. I turned to Ava and mouthed, *"I'm headed downstairs!"* Ava's eyes lit up and the smile on her face matched.

As Brad and I approached the top of the stairs, a subtle but real fear tightened in my gut. Halting at the top step, I braced myself as I always do when faced with the challenge of walking downstairs in four-inch heels. I surveyed the twenty-plus potential kiss-of-death steps below me, and began, as elegantly as possible, to accomplish the dreaded task of making it to the bottom unscathed. In situations such as this, I prefer a sturdy railing to grip and steady legs, not these loosey-gooseys that were trembling just from being next to him.

"Where does Ava live?" Brad asked like someone *not* terrified about getting from point A to point B in one piece. I gripped his arm tightly and held him back from going any further than the five steps we had successfully taken.

"Confession time, Brad. See this seven-inch beauty mark?" I held my right leg out like I was doing the Can-Can, showing off the scar that ran down the front of my knee. "This little badge of honor makes me a bit of a weenie about stairs," I smiled up at him. "I'll consider all questions when we reach the bottom safely."

As if my outstretched leg was an invitation to be touched, Brad's free hand took the liberty of holding onto it, just under my calf muscle. My stomach fluttered as I willed my leg to stop shaking from his touch. "Wow, that's a nasty scar," he said examining my knee. "You must really dislike stairs. You're shaking."

I pulled my lips in, staring straight ahead and contemplated whether or not to confess the stairs weren't the only cause of my leg tremors.

As Brad is not a priest, I decided against it.

"I can't wait to hear what led to that, but first, let's get you down these stairs unharmed," he said, gently releasing my leg. I re-engaged the death grip I had on his arm, and we continued our descent.

"Did you actually say 'weenie'?"

"Stop talking to me Brad," I sing-songed.

Brad chuckled, not saying another word until we made it safely to the main floor.

"She lives on Congress, I think? You can see the capitol from her apartment."

Brad stopped abruptly, looking at me inquisitively. "Oh!" he exclaimed, like, he could have had a V-8! "I had no idea what you were talking about. I completely forgot I had asked you where she lives. The whole weenie thing threw me off."

All I could do was shove my embarrassment into a side-lipped grin.

* * *

Leading me by the hand to the now-packed downstairs bar, Brad directed me to stand in front of him, positioning himself very close behind me as we waited in line. The rise and fall of his chest rhythmically brushed against my back with every inhale. My ears flushed hot as my breathing fell in line with his, growing deeper and heavier. I watched as my double-Ds rose and fell with every breath the two of us synced together. Terrified of doing to the man standing in front of me what Brad was doing to me, I rounded my shoulders, causing my back to be in full contact with Brad's chest. *I could orgasm right here and now.* And if him breathing wasn't enough to send me over the edge, his hands were. Firm against my forearms, they slid slowly up the sides of my arms, giving me little squeezes along the way.

"You have really soft skin," he said over my shoulder. I closed my eyes and smiled. Just the weight of his hands on my shoulders filled me with butterflies. With the bar now more crowded, Brad bumped against me as people infringed on him from behind. His stance firmed, protecting me, but as he did, I felt him, *that* part of him, at the small of my back. *Nice, Delores,* clitoris's pseudonym thought, as she quivered inside my panties. *Calm down, sister,* I cautioned her silently.

Brad leaned his head close to mine and tenderly moved my hair away from my ear. With his other hand on the back of my neck and his thumb slightly behind my ear, he turned my head toward his. "What would you like to drink?" he asked. The vibration of his voice leaving me weak. *Oh. Mah. Gah ... Yes, I will go home with you! Yes, I will marry you!*

24

Babies? I thought I was done, but for you? These are the thoughts that raced through my mind as goosebumps raced down my neck and throughout my body, spreading as fast as wildfire in July. I blinked a few times, working to redirect my thoughts away from his lips and *that* part of him that was touching the top of my ass.

I swallowed hard, clearing my throat, "Grey Goose 7-up, tall, please," I answered, abandoning the grape-flavored vodka I'd been drinking all night, concerned he might think it was a little too girly. Which it probably was. The guy in front of us left with his drinks and I scooted forward to the bar with Brad close behind. Up close, the bar was much taller than it seemed when I first walked in, its edge lining up just under my breasts. Brad leaned around me, resting his arm on the bar while the hand on my neck traveled down my spine, landing at the small of my back.

His touch was dizzying.

Intentional and slow.

Yielding yet possessive.

I looked down at his hand that was resting on the bar. I liked that it didn't look like a hand that belonged to someone younger. Brad had manly man hands. Despite them feeling soft against my skin, they also looked weathered, like he wasn't afraid of getting them dirty. I hoped to see just how dirty they could get.

"Two Grey Goose 7-ups, … tall, please," Brad ordered our drinks from the bartender, who repeated it back. Brad nodded, then turned and gave me another wink. I don't know why, but a wink like that from a man I find attractive really gets me. It's like our own private Morse code: *I think you're hot. I want only you. With this wink you're mine, because it's intimate, shared only between us.* His wink sent an aftershock of giddiness through my body. Resuming his stance behind me, more aftershocks followed as his hand made its way back up to my neck. Tilting my head toward his as he'd done before, I leaned back against him, eager to hear him speak against my ear and into my soul. As I waited, Brad's lips brushed lightly across my ear and I closed my eyes, relishing how good it felt with him so close. Then his lips met mine unexpectedly, stealing a kiss.

Oh Gawd! Every part of me was weak, like a limp noodle. Brad seemed unfazed as he reached in front of me to retrieve our drinks. With his focus elsewhere, I shook my head like someone was waving smelling salts under my nose. *Pull yourself together, sister! You got this! This is not your first rodeo, not by any stretch of the imagination ... It's just been a long, long, long, long, long time since your last time in the saddle.* Even Brad's voice and the way he spoke with the bartender was sexy. I clenched my teeth, feeling the muscles in my jaw pulse as he turned and looked at me, causing my heart to skip, yet again ... *I think I'm ready to get back on that horse.*

* * *

Brad handed me my drink and led me away from all the noise and the crowd to the long table in the other room. It was weirdly less crowded in here, maybe because the upstairs bar was outside. This room reminded me of an intimate speakeasy. Brad directed me to an available barstool, which faced another.

"I should let Ava know we're going to stay down here," I said, hesitating before I sat down.

"I've got it," he assured me. Using the hand holding his drink, he pointed toward the stairs and nodded his head in their direction. "I have a straight view of the stairs. When she comes down, I'll see her."

Not being able to pick his friend Greg out of a crowd of three, in this moment his answer was good enough for me.

"So, Ms. Lake from Denver, Colorado, tell me more about why you're in Austin," he inquired with a look of actual interest.

As I explained the very uncomplicated reason for my visit, I found it hard to concentrate as my eyes fixed on Brad's lips that were silently screaming *Do you see how more beautiful we are face to face?* To their point, I did. And to make matters worse, Brad set his drink on the table to my right, allowing his now-free hand to land lightly on the outside of my knee. I gazed down at the hand caressing my leg. Such a foreign thing for me to see at this stage in my twenty-two-month dry spell. (I guess I can't really call it a dry spell when it's by choice. At this point in my life, I was choosing to save myself for marriage. Yes, you read that right. So far, the too-many-to-count relationships that started off with sex clearly hadn't worked, so I was trying something new. *Saving myself.* To be honest, this tactic wasn't exactly working out either.) Before I could get a grasp on hotness here touching my knee, he slid his bar stool forward. I looked down to see our legs had become entwined. Someone here had longer legs than I did. One more inch and his knee would be under my dress. Having something, nay someone, this close to me … the muscles in my legs tensed, squeezing what was sandwiched between them. Desperately, I tried to stay on track with the conversation. Brad scooted his barstool closer, and I glanced down just in time to see his knee disappear under my dress, where it now rested inches from Delores. My head felt light, like a helium-filled balloon as Brad continued asking me about myself, laughing at things I said, while still caressing and squeezing my knee. As I listened to Brad talk, the sound of his voice, the feel of his touch, the way he looked into my eyes … the helium dizzied me. Preoccupied by all things Brad, he leaned into me, at last bringing his lips to mine once again. His tongue entered my mouth, warm and soft. My soul melted into his as his lips and his tongue mixed fluidly with mine. I held onto his thigh, feeling his muscles tighten under his jeans, my hand supporting me as our bodies met halfway. Our tongues explored and I pictured an ocean, a wave exploding as it smashes against a large rock. Kissing him was euphoric, tingling my insides as if they were on the downhill side of a roller coaster. It had been so long since I had allowed anyone to be this intimate with me. I was deaf to the music playing overhead as the only song I could hear in my head was "Mr. Brightside" by The Killers. *"It started out with a kiss… It was only a kiss…"* But this wasn't *only* a kiss. This was a kiss with a stranger, someone new, a kiss without any pain or baggage attached to it.

Every so often, I would pull away from him for safe measure, fearful that if I didn't, I might devour him. During these breaks Brad rested his forehead against mine, whispering or chuckling things to me like, "That's hot" or "God, you taste good."

His breath was warm against my lips and smelled of alcohol, taking me back to high school and the first time I noticed liquor on someone's breath. Having grown up in a strict religious household, the smell of alcohol was not something I had been familiar with. Brad's scent took me back to the first time I kissed my high school boyfriend after he'd been out drinking with his friends. It surprised me, how sexy and dangerous I felt back then. I closed my eyes and breathed in the light scent of whatever it was Brad had been drinking before we met, grateful at the sweet and distant memory it brought.

✳ ✳ ✳

Brad and I continued to talk, touch, and kiss for what was probably an hour, but felt like only minutes. He was recently divorced with three kids, and when he told me what he did for a living (something to do with computer chips) I congratulated him on having found a cure for insomnia. When someone asks what I do for a living, the explanation is simple: I do hair. When someone tries to explain computer chips to me, my eyes glaze over. Laughing at my insomnia comment, Brad looked past me to the stairs. "Your friend? Ava? Right?"

"I'm sorry? Ava who?" I smirked. Brad laughed again. *God! Even his laugh is sexy.*

"She's coming down the stairs."

I glanced over my shoulder and saw Ava, just as Brad had promised, and marveled at his superpower of having met her only once and yet being able to recognize her an hour later. As Ava made eye contact with me, my eyes grew wide, and I tucked my lips inward to keep from smiling as she reached the last step.

"There you are!" she exclaimed, walking over to us. "And what have you two been up to?" she asked in her notorious laugh-as-she-talked voice.

"Just makin' out!" I reported, unable to hide my smile any longer. Brad chuckled and asked Ava what she had been up to.

"Just waitin' for ya'll to get to know each other." Looking us up and down she added, "I see that's happened?" By the time she was able to spit out the last word, she was in a full-on laugh. "So, I'm ready to head home." Pausing, and raising her eyebrows, she continued, "Are you two coming?"

chapter 3

Ava knew about my quest for no-sex-till-I-find-the-one. She had even poked fun at me on the way out that night, casually commenting, "And if you bring someone back with you tonight, please keep it quiet, Booboo. The walls in my apartment are paper-thin!" The two of us laughed ourselves silly at the very thought of me breaking my quest. And get this! This wasn't my first attempt at celibacy.

The time before this lasted eighteen months. I broke that promise to myself with the greatest guy ... he wanted all the same things in life that I did. How do I know this? He told me so. And I believed him. Did I believe he was my perfect match? Not really. Did I believe we were equally yoked? Nope. Was I one hundred percent attracted to him? Not at all. What I *was,* was tired. Tired of the dating scene. Tired of online dating. Tired of being set up with men that my friends assured me were perfect for me, only to find that the *only* thing we had in common was that we were both single. So, when this last guy, who was shorter than me by a good inch (even though he claimed he was five-foot-ten), matched me almost perfectly on Match.com, I decided I needed to let go of his lie about his height, as well as his lie about having an athletic build (he was chunky, complete with man boobs ... yes, *moobs*), and give him a chance. I mean, according to this dating site, we *matched.* After five months of dating exclusively and having sex because we were "exclusive," I caught that five-foot-six, fat-moobed-liar red-handed at his house with another woman. After many tears (on my part; he had a guest waiting) and countless "Whys?" without an answer, I collected the few belongings I had at his house and left, but not before his dog, you know, man's best friend, ran from the house and straight to my car. After several failed attempts at calling his dog back, he had to walk out to my car, barefoot in the snow, and drag him back to his house by the collar.

You see, I had been *that* sweet girl, the one who watched that fucker's dog for him when he traveled. As sweet as the dog's attempt to escape with me was, I am positive it wasn't as sweet as his parting gift to me. *Trichomoniasis*. Or, in layman's terms, *Trich*. Yep, that asshole turned my gyna (aka my vag, aka vagina) into what I can only describe as smelling like someone had left one hundred open cans of tuna in a black car on a one-hundred-twenty-degree day, complete with an itch that would make a mosquito proud.

And now here we were, me, Ava, and Brad, in the back seat of a cab, making our way to Ava's. I mean, what the *fuck* was I thinking?

* * *

Ava and Brad talked the entire drive as I sat between them, watching, like I wasn't even there, an out-of-body experience, if you will. My head swiveled from Brad to Ava and then back to Brad, like I was watching a tennis match at Wimbledon.

Arriving outside Ava's apartment, Brad paid for the cab. There wasn't any hesitation about who was paying. As soon as we pulled up, chivalrous Brad had cash in hand and was thanking the driver. *It's the little things.* And me? I had come down with a case of cat-got-your-tongue. I couldn't speak. Luckily, Ava and Brad continued chatting for the two-minute walk from the street to Ava's apartment. Once inside, the three of us huddled together in her small foyer. Knowing the drill, I steadied myself on Brad's arm, also feeling the muscle of his bicep under his shirt. *Delicious.* I reached down with my other hand and gripped the heel of my shoe, wiggling it side to side as I struggled to pry it from my sweaty foot. A sound like cranberry jelly slurping out of a can at Thanksgiving escaped as my Sam Edelman released my foot from its grasp. Ava mirrored me as she held onto the wall, coaxing her heels to do the same.

"Brad?" Ava said, looking over at the two of us. "This is where we get to see the real you! Hope you don't have any holes in your socks!"

I spun around to face the door, hoping to hide the blush in my cheeks. *Please, God, no holes*, I prayed while holding onto him with my other hand as I struggled with my other heel.

Brad however, easily slipped out of his brown oxfords. *Men.*

"I'm good," he began. "I was brought up to never leave the house with dirty underwear. Or holey socks." Relief swept over me. Socks with holes in them is a pet peeve of mine, unfortunately, one of many.

Footwear off, Ava, always the perfect hostess, led us down the short hallway and into the kitchen. "Here are the glasses," she said, opening a cabinet. She retrieved three drinking glasses, then showed us where the filtered water was in the fridge. "Ya'll need anything else?" she asked filling her glass with water.

"I think we're good?" I shrugged, unsure. I looked to Brad for confirmation.

"Any chance you have some ibuprofen?" he asked.

"Ah, good thinking," Ava said. She reached into the pantry and pulled out the save-yourself-from-a-hangover pills, swallowed two down, and left us. She didn't say a word as she went straight to her room, closed the door, and locked it!

And there I was … alone with Brad for the first time. Gulp.

"Well, that was a fast exit!" Brad laughed.

"I'm sure she's just a little skerd," I smiled up at him, handing him one of the glasses I had filled with water.

"Are you? What did you say … *skerd?*" he asked, offering me two ibuprofens. Taking the capsules from him, I placed them on my tongue and drank them down, my eyes never leaving his.

"I think," I took a breath, walking past him to the hallway, "I might be too nervous to be scared," I smiled at him over my shoulder as I led him back down the hall to the guest room.

"You're nervous?"

"A little, if I'm being honest. I mean," I shrugged, allowing him to fill in the blank. Inside the room, I watched as he closed the door behind him, never turning away from me.

"Well, I don't want you to be nervous." He said, stepping closer, now standing between the queen-size bed and armoire. The guest room wasn't spacious, but for an apartment it was impressive. Brad set his water on top of the armoire.

"Is that on a coaster or something?" I winced.

Brad smiled. "Yes. There is a coaster, and I am using it."

"Thank you." My cheeks flushed with embarrassment at the insinuation that he was raised in a barn.

"I see why you asked," he said, looking me up and down. "How many inches were on those heels you were wearing? You're kind of short."

"I am not short!" I retorted, faking my offense. "I'm five-foot-seven!" My hands reverted to the *Price Is Right* as I showcased my frame. "Not tall, I'll give you that, but not short either," I surrendered. And just like that, my nervousness disappeared and the ease I felt earlier that night with him wafted over me, as did the seductive scent of his cologne. "How tall are you, by the way?" I asked, wondering if I was close in my initial assumption.

"Six-three."

"Makes sense that you can see up there. I like how tall you are."

"I like how tall I am, too." He smiled. I wanted to melt into his voice. God it was soothing. I wished I had a way to record it so I could replay this luxuriousness during my home-alone masturbating sessions.

"*Soooooo*, this is the room where the magic happens," I said, making light, changing the subject.

Brad looked around. "Poor Ava."

"Oh my gosh, you did not just say," but Brad interrupted me with his lips and the excitement I'd felt with him at the bar returned. Soft and full, his lips were still new yet growing more familiar with each kiss. Kissing him felt like home, comfortable, safe, warm, and inviting. His hands slid down to my hips, his thumbs caressing my hip bones as his fingers held tight to my lower back, guiding me closer to him. I don't think a man's hands have ever suited my body more perfectly. I loved how strong they were. *Never have I ever* felt so dainty; dainty felt good.

Reluctantly I pulled away from his lips, desperate to ditch my water so I could reciprocate his hands-on-ed-ness. As I turned toward the nightstand, I heard a soft knock at the door, followed by the sound of something being shoved under it. Ava giggled from the other side, and seconds later I heard her bedroom door close again.

"What was that?" I asked. Brad walked over to investigate.

Chuckling, Brad bent over to pick up whatever it was Ava had shoved under the door. "Little presumptuous of her?" Blood rushed to my cheeks as Brad held up not one, but *two* condoms. Don't get me wrong, my intentions were not to keep this G-rated. But two condoms? *R-rated, party of two, please.*

"Thank God for good, safe friends," I said, trying to sound nonchalant while also trying to hide my embarrassment. I turned toward the nightstand again, placed my glass on a coaster, and attached my iPod to the speaker. Scrolling through my playlists, I found and clicked "Chill." First song up was The Eagles' "Best of My Love." Glenn Frey's acoustic guitar strummed the familiar tune I'd known most of my life, taking me back to the mid-1970s and the countless evenings my mom drove our carpool home from swim practice. Exhausted from the usual 5,000-yard practice, I'd quietly settle in the backseat of her cherry red Chevy Nova.

Winters in Utah where I grew up were cold and snowy, and as the windows fogged from the warmth of our bodies, I would quietly draw hearts on the glass, watching as the night sky shone through the tracings of my index finger. With each heart, I would dream of the day someone would love me the way the singer from The Eagles loved the woman in this song. Reminiscing, I smiled. I had to have been seven when this song came out. I don't think there was ever a time I didn't want to be in love like that.

"This is a great song," Brad said, inches away from me.

"It's probably my most favorite Eagles song," I said, my voice sounding a little hoarse from who knows what. Maybe it was Brad standing so close to me, looking at me the way he was in the dimly lit room, not yet touching me, combined with the ambiance of the song. Then Brad invaded my space even more, his fingers softly tracing the sides of my hairline. Chills raced up my neck, through my scalp, and back down my spine. I was swimming in a sea of lightheadedness as Brad tenderly brushed his hands through my hair, cupping the back of my head in his hands, while Don Henley continued breaking my heart with his words. I tilted my face up toward his, wanting his lips on mine once again, so I invited him in. Soft yet full of passion, his lips met mine as his hands, firm behind my head, pulled me closer, his thumbs gently caressing the sides of my jaw. With our lips connected and tongues exploring each other, I watched once again as my tiny index finger drew hearts of hope on my mom's foggy car windows. I was grateful for this moment of being with Brad, but at the same time, a tinge of sadness crept in. I felt sad for her, the little girl who had never realized what she had always hoped she would. Brad's hands moved to the back of my dress, snapping me and my attention back to this moment as he tugged on the tongue of my zipper.

"Ouch! My hair is stuck." I whispered, hoping to conceal the pain of zipper-stuck hair strands. I lifted the remaining unstuck hair into a makeshift ponytail and turned my back to him offering him the opportunity to get me unstuck.

"Sorry about that," he said, grazing his lips against my now exposed neck. *God, my neck!* Another surge of chills washed over me. Patiently and impressively, Brad released my hair and teased the freed zipper down my spine to the small of my back. As my dress fell away, I released my hair. Brad slipped his hands inside the back of my dress, pushing it off my shoulders. His thumbs, soft from years of computer work, silhouetted down the sides of my arms, my wrists, and then my hands until there was nothing more than my blue lace bra covering my torso.

I melted my back against his chest and a sigh of contentment escaped me. Brad lifted my hair from between us, leaving just the fabric of his shirt against my bare skin. I opened my neck and shoulders to him, inviting his lips once again. I loved being here with him and closed my eyes as I sought to capture this moment in my sweetest of memories. Locking away how my body responded to his touch, reeling like I had jumped off a forty-foot cliff at Lake Powell into the darkness of night without knowing how far the water lay below. Locking away the sensation I felt from the warmth of his breath as it danced over my skin. I had waited so long to feel someone's lips softly kiss my neck, or to experience the chills that would invade my skin as someone seduced me for the first time.

Brad's lips trailed from my neck to my shoulder, his tongue lightly licking my skin before nibbling gently, causing me to inhale sharply. I tilted my face to his, begging his lips back to mine, Brad accepted. *God, this felt good...he felt good.*

I wanted to face him but didn't want to stop kissing him and tried turning my body to his, but the connection was lost. "You are ridiculously sexy. You know that right?" he said, flattering me.

Although I *felt* sexy in this moment, I would never admit to *knowing* I was sexy, let alone ridiculously sexy. That was just silly. I didn't answer. I couldn't. I was too taken with him. *God, he was beautiful*, I thought, looking up into his dark-blue eyes, eyes that were hungrily staring back into mine.

Unable to look away, blood flushed and pulsed in my cheeks. It was somewhat flustering to hold his gaze this long, but now it was a game of chicken and I refused to be the first to look away. As the game progressed, neither of us moving, my desire to kiss him overwhelmed me. A good reason to end the game that only I was playing. I rose on my tiptoes, laced my fingers behind his neck, and, at my lead, our lips reconnected. Brad, having been in control, pressed his lips to mine, his tongue riveting, licking the line between my lips as his tongue teased to be inside my mouth. I pulled away so I could take in his lips and the freshly shaven skin around them, staring long enough for him to know how much I wanted them. Moving back in, my tongue teased his lips, mimicking what he had done to me. I traced the line between his lips and smiled as he let out a soft moan. His arms wrapped around my waist, pulling me in tight, his tongue prodding me as something down below pressed hard against me. Ah, the pleasure I would experience from what was down there, Delores throbbed, wanting nothing more than to know what he would feel like.

I slid my hands from his neck to the front of his shirt, feeling my way blindly, his mouth entangled with mine as I undid each button. Echoing the way he had removed my dress, I slipped my hands inside the top part of his shirt. "Two shirts?" I breathed into his mouth, feeling a t-shirt under his button-down. "Not fair."

Brad smiled against my lips, still kissing me, as I removed his shirt from his shoulders, silhouetting my thumbs down his arms as he had done to me. Brad let out another soft moan as goosebumps spread down his arms. A smile escaped us both, and as my hands reached his forearms, his shirt tumbled to the floor.

Then I looked to his t-shirt, disappointed at all the work I had to put in, but as I tugged to release it from being tucked, I decided a t-shirt would be far easier to remove than my bra would be. Untucked, I slid his shirt up his stomach and as Brad lifted his arms to help me, I stood face to face with perfection. *Good God!* He was ab-so-lutely beautiful!

Had I not known any better, I would have thought he was a Calvin Klein model, broad chest, broad shoulders, lats, a six-pack. *Thank you, God,* I prayed silently.

I was distracted by what was in front of me, so Brad finished removing his t-shirt and my fingers trickled down his chest slowly. An explosion of goosebumps emerged and continued as my fingers floated ... *bump ... bump ... bump ...* lightly down his washboard.

A forced breath rushed from my lungs. Unaware I'd been holding it, I stared, trance-like, beholding his perfection. I inhaled slowly, eagerly watching as my fingers glided past the sides of his belly button and down to the best spot in the world. A man's sweet spot, the spot between hip bones and lower stomach. That V that leads to all things wonderful. Brad lifted my chin with his finger, forcing my gaze away from heaven. Looking up, I was unable to decide which was more beautiful: his face or his body? Great thing was, I didn't have to choose. Eyes reconnected, I tried, and failed, to hide my attitude-of-gratitude giddiness, but a sigh of admiration betrayed me. I sucked several quick sips of air before biting my lip, hoping the pain inflicted by my teeth would stop exposing me. But it was no use. I was busted ... the smile on Brad's face said he was busted too.

Meshing our smiles back into a slow, tantalizing kiss, I willed my hands to leave his stomach, directing them to something new. His belt. As I tugged at the strap, Brad reached behind me, effortlessly unhooking the back of my bra. *Well, that wasn't so difficult.* I thought, comparing it to the removal of his t-shirt and his oxfords. *Men.*

Brad gently massaged the line where my bra strap had been. Igniting more chills than I thought possible, he caressed my back, and his hands made their way up to my shoulders, where he gently grasped my bra straps. I wanted to look into his eyes as he removed my bra and broke away from his kiss. *So much for holding his gaze,* I thought, my eyes closing involuntarily as the lace from my bra slid slowly down my nipples until it came to rest at my wrists. I opened my eyes, licking my lips slowly, adoring the way his eyes were feasting on my exposed breasts.

"Mommy," he joked, smiling down at them, biting on one of his knuckles. His goofiness made me smile even more. His belt, however, was starting to piss me off. It was worn and set in its ways and was taking a good amount of effort to reveal what was behind its grooves.

A few tugs more and his belt was finally undone. Next up: the button of his jeans. To my relief and good fortune, there was zero resistance. Moving on to his zipper, Brad pulled away, leaving my hands empty, allowing my bra to fall from my wrists to the floor.

* * *

Through the speaker, "The Best of My Love" ended and Rusted Root's "Beautiful People" began as I, determined, reached for his zipper again. Brad put his index finger under my chin once more, lifting it, directing my gaze away from what I hoped to see behind that zipper and into his eyes. Shaking his head, *no*, Brad smirked, the smirk I'd seen earlier at the bar, the smirk that I was quickly finding endearing. Bending down toward my breasts, Brad cupped them in his hands, and I watched as he kissed my right nipple, taking it in his mouth briefly. A long, deep inhale filled my lungs, pushing my breasts closer to him, while a wave of unsteadiness flooded me, watching him enjoy me.

Lost in his lips and where they were, Brad wrapped his arm around my mid-back and, as if I weighed nothing, lifted me, like Superman with Lois Lane, onto the bed, gently laying me on the duvet cover. He stood; eyes connected; he penetrated my soul. Brad was a stranger, a stranger who was giving me a connection I'd longed for … for … forever. He slowly unzipped his pants, teasing me, never taking his eyes from mine. Smirking his smirk, Brad shimmied his pants until they fell to the floor, exposing black-and-grey striped boxer briefs and the hard contents hidden inside. *Thank you, God … again.*

Pants-less, Brad crawled onto the bed, hovering on all fours above me. "You really are beautiful," he said. Hearing these words from him, flooded my heart with elation. It had been so long since I'd allowed myself to be this close to a man, let alone heard anything intimately sweet said to me. I felt like a 1940s actress, swooning.

"Thank you," I said. My eyes fluttered slightly, matching my breath as I shyly dodged his gaze. With his weight on his elbows, Brad hovered closer to me, just above my mouth, breathing me in before pressing his lips against mine. I took in the fullness of his bottom lip and sucked it gently. Kissing him was effortless. With every movement of his head, his tongue, and his lips … my body sparked, full of life.

Mazzy Star's "Fade into You" began to play, and I couldn't have picked a more perfect song to hold this moment in my memory. Slowly, my fingertips touched his arms, his back, trickling down to his perfect ass still covered in his boxers. I wanted to memorize every part of him, using my hands, eyes, and lips. I hoped to keep this moment with him locked away for safekeeping. Slowly, methodically, Brad kissed my cheek, my jaw, the side of my neck … I allowed my eyes to close, savoring every kiss, not knowing where the next would land … the front of my neck, slowly moving down my chest to the left, then the right, then center, and then to my breasts now tingling as he kissed and teased me with his mouth and tongue.

I opened my eyes and stared up at the ceiling… *I mean it, God. Thank you. Thank you for this.* Brad continued kissing, nibbling, teasing the underside of my right breast, my ribs, and then my stomach as I squirmed with anticipation. And then he stopped. Sitting back on his haunches, Brad looked down at my dress that was still at my waist, then gently pulled it down over my hips, simultaneously backing himself off the bed. Kneeling down on the floor in front of me, he freed my legs until the garment lay on the ground with the rest of our clothes. Only two articles of clothing remained between us. With my dress discarded, Brad knelt closer to the bed, wriggling himself between my legs, spreading them apart as he did. I reached over my head and grabbed the top of the duvet cover, pulling it under my head and below my shoulders. "Will you help me move this?" I asked. "If anything were to get on the cover, I would die." Brad smiled and assisted me, pulling the part of the duvet closest to him out from under my legs. He folded it and put it at the foot of the bed.

"You're a good houseguest," he grinned, resuming his spot between my legs.

"I don't know about that," I deadpanned. "I did bring a stranger into Ava's home."

"Touché." He nodded with a smile as he looked down at my legs. Shaking his head slightly, he inhaled slowly, looking like a kid who had been given an entire chocolate cake to eat … all by himself. Speaking of eating … Brad kissed the insides of my thighs, sending a surge of fight, flight, or freeze through my stomach at the touch of his lips. Playfully, he kissed my legs, looking at my expression after each kiss as his lips brought him closer to *that* place. His mouth, now at my panties, sent a warmth of breath through the fabric, conquering their post of protection. I gripped the bedsheets as he pressed his mouth into me, biting my panties, pulling them away with his teeth.

"Oh, my … gawd," I exhaled. But the pleasure I was experiencing was short lived as Brad wrapped his fingers around the sides of my panties. Panic set in and I jolted up on my elbows, pushing him away as I pulled my feet to the edge of the bed. I knocked my knees together, "So, I …" Hesitating, I tipped my legs to the side so I could see his face. Brad looked confused … and with good reason. My sudden movements seemed to have startled him and he stared at me, eyebrows raised.

"Yes?" he asked curiously,

"So, I… God, this is embarrassing!" I exhaled, shaking my head *no*. Accepting my fate, I looked him square in the eyes, and blurted out, "I have been celibate for," I hesitated again, "some time now." This clearly set him back ... *and with good reason!*

"Oh?" The look on his face seemed to be one of pure disbelief. "Is that so?"

"Yes, and I ..." I lay back on the bed, wondering if I should let him behind the curtain. *Did he need to know my deepest secrets and desires? Where's the harm? I'll probably never see this man again ...* as that realization set in, I knew I didn't want the cloud of waiting for *the one* hanging over this moment. Because in this moment, I no longer cared to wait. "I mean, I guess I wouldn't call it celibate, right? It's just that, I don't know." I flustered. *Flustered is what you get for not being honest.* "It's just been a long time since anyone has been *down* there." I tipped my head back against the bed. Deflated, I waited for his response.

"Oh!" he said again, sitting back on his heels. "How long has it been? If you don't mind me asking."

My mouth twisted to the side. "Twenty-two months." Hearing it out loud, I realized just how absurd it sounded. Propping myself back up on my elbows I continued, "And it's not that I'm not up for this ... at all." My hands were talking as much as my mouth as I nervously and quickly tried to explain, but not explain, my situation. "I am up for it," I rambled, hoping to reassure him, "*very* up for it. It's just that," I exhaled audibly, forcibly plopping my body back on the bed, bringing my knees back up from their tilted position. "It's just that, I'm a little unruly down there ... it's embarrassing," I said, covering my eyes with my hands. I waited in silence, listening for the sound of the door as he left. Hearing nothing, I lifted a couple fingers, and peeked out. Brad was still there, watching me with an amused expression.

"I'm not worried about it. Unless you are?" he added, looking at me with the sweetest shit-eating grin.

I pushed back up on my elbows so we could talk face to face. "Kind of. I mean … I pride myself on my maintenance. But with zero activity as of late, I believe it's gotten a little out of hand."

Brad started to laugh and knelt back up to the edge of the bed. Coaxing my legs so they were once again straddling him, he kissed his way, in slow small increments beginning at my knees, crawling back on top of me and kissing me until he reached my face. "I'm not worried," he said. Brad's voice knew no boundaries as it penetrated every nook and cranny of my being. "You let me know what you're comfortable with."

I couldn't help but fall in more *like* with him, and how kind he was. I didn't know him, but in this moment, he was everything I ever wanted in a man. He was sweet, he was fun, he was honest, he was respectful, he was good. I decided then and there that I would never know anything different of him. I wouldn't allow myself to. With my past experiences in mind, I knew that knowing someone, letting them behind the curtain, allowing myself to be vulnerable with them also meant being hurt by them. By all accounts, Brad was the perfect model of the Mr. Right, I'd been longing for, and the best damn Mr. Right *Now*, I could have hoped for.

"I'm good with this." I surrendered, my toes sliding up, caressing the sides of his legs. "Definitely more than good." My hands lightly tickled up the sides of his arms. "I just had to give you a disclaimer."

The faint instrumentals of "Dig" by Incubus came through the speaker as Brad continued. "Disclaimer noted. Now, where was I?" he asked, pushing himself up as he looked down at my panties. "Ah, yes. I remember." Looking to me, Brad silently confirmed my permission. I smiled, biting my lip nervously. Permission granted. Grinning at me, he laced my panties around his fingers and gave them a little tug, causing me to flinch.

"Sorry," I grimaced. Taking a deep breath, I willed myself to relax. Thankfully, I'm good at self-talk and was able to let go of my unnecessary embarrassment. Brad, seemingly unaware of the wrestling match going on inside my head, continued backing off the bed, taking my dark-blue Hanky Pankys with him. With my panties to my knees, he deliberately looked down at my now exposed jungle and then back to me.

"This is what you were worried about?" he questioned, standing at the edge of the bed. He let out a sigh and shook his head, letting me know I had nothing to be embarrassed about. I watched as his gaze drifted down to my legs, then up to my stomach and then my face, "You're beautiful," he said admiringly, looking like he was the one now inhaling smelling salts. I loved how deep and, at times, inaudible, his voice was. I grew more and more wet with every compliment. Uncomfortable and flattered, I whispered "Thank you," while silently thanking my past self for years of swim and yoga practices … and painful Brazilians. As I lay there with him looking at me, listening to him pour sweet nothings over me, a dichotomy of feelings stirred: embarrassment, desire, anxiousness, and excitement. Brad brought the feelings of desire and excitement to the forefront as he lured my panties past my toes to where they fell, joining the rest of the yard sale next to the bed.

Back on the bed, Brad crawled over me, like a predator over his prey. "You are absolutely gorgeous," he breathed into my neck, his voice thick and sexy. My back arched involuntarily, positioning me closer to him as his mouth found its way from my neck to my chest. "Gorgeous and sexy," he continued, his voice now reverberating between my breasts. Teasing me, he kissed my right breast, flicking my nipple lightly with his tongue. A moan resounded in my throat and my lungs pushed my breasts closer to his mouth, begging him for more. Brad left me begging as he continued teasing me, his lips leaving where I so desperately wanted them to stay as they trailed down my torso.

With one hand firm at my waist, the other gripped my thigh as his lips sprinkled kisses over my stomach. It was heavenly having him here, holding me, kissing me. "God, I love your body." His words warmed my skin as he continued his descent, dragging his tongue across my lower abdomen causing it to ripple like a wave.

I lifted my head to watch as his lips left my stomach and descended lower. Knowing where he was headed but not yet ready, I grabbed his shoulders and gently pushed him away from me. Brad took my direction and backed himself off the bed, then stood at its edge. Light from the bedside lamp illuminated his body, giving me just enough light by which to see him. Combined with the glow from the outdoor security lamps that peeped through the blinds behind me, the pleasure of looking at his beautiful body was all mine. I snailed my way to the edge of the bed until my legs dangled over the side and the balls of my feet firmed themselves against one of the discarded pieces of clothes that were piled on the floor.

I smiled coyly up at Brad as my fingers danced their way along the waistband of his boxers. A million thoughts raced through my mind; nervousness mixed with excitement. *Am I seriously here right now? Is this really about to happen? This is probably going to hurt my jaw!* Blood surged hot through my cheeks and ears as I tugged at his waistband, exposing *him*. I heard my breath grow heavier, more labored, like it wasn't even mine, and I felt faint. And then, I licked *him* like an ice cream cone. *What the eff, Lake? Who are you right now?* But before I could answer myself, Brad moaned, coaxing a desire within me. Looking down at *him,* my heart pounded as it worked double-time pumping blood through my veins. Somewhere in all of this, Brad's boxers made their way to the floor; I had no idea which of us had made that happen, nor did I care. I swallowed hard, gathered my courage, then put my lips around him. *Yes,* I sighed, relieved, *just like riding a bike.*

Brad moaned again, throatily, and gripped my hair in his fingers. "Lake! I'm getting lightheaded," he said, swaying slightly.

"Pun intended?" I asked teasingly, gazing up.

"God, you're hot." Brad's eyes penetrated my soul as he looked down at me, instilling in me a greater lust and desire for him ... *all* of him, but before I could have my way, Brad tugged at my hair to stop me.

"Too much teeth?" I grimaced with embarrassment.

"What?" he asked, looking disheveled. "Oh! God, no!" he exclaimed, my question seeping in. Brad took my face in his hands as he bent down toward me. "That was amazing. You're amazing," he reassured, kissing me. "But if you keep that up, I'm not going to last. It's my turn."

"Your turn?" I asked, feeling a bit cheated. "Okay, but just to be clear, I don't feel like that was much of a turn." Brad tilted his head to the side, raising an eyebrow in a yeah-that's-probably-true sort of way and playfully pushed me back on the bed, causing me to laugh. I scooted further back and settled in against the soft, cool bed sheets, making a mental note to ask Ava where she had purchased them. Brad knelt back down at the edge of the bed and began kissing my legs again. I stuffed a pillow under my head so I could watch him, which was just as sexy as feeling the warmth of his tongue as it licked, kissed, and nibbled the insides of my thighs.

Brad took his time, kissing my thighs like he was creating a treasure map. I closed my eyes as his lips made their way to where X marked the spot. I tried closing my legs as nervousness beat out anticipation, but Brad held them firm where they were.

"Uh-uh," He smiled shaking his head *no* at me, "it's my turn, remember?" I swallowed hard, willed myself to relax, and inhaled a slow, deep breath. "And I plan to take my time," he continued, dragging his lips against my upper thighs. My face flushed again as I caught him looking up at me. As nervous as I was having him so close to my lack of maintenance, Brad didn't seem to care at all and continued tormenting my inner thighs with his kisses. I resisted the urge to buck my hips up to his mouth and invite him in. The feeling of helium that had filled my head at the bar reappeared as Brad deposited more kisses along my thighs, dangerously close to where I longed for him to be.

Brad adjusted himself further up the bed. *So close and yet so far.* I tangled my hands in his hair and saw Brad look up at me as his shoulders nudged my thighs further apart. Legs where he wanted them, Brad looked down at his treasure, the very place my eyes had been urging his mouth to go. And go it went, pressing against me. Brad moaned like he'd been the celibate one.

With his tongue pressed against me, my eyes rolled and closed as my head pushed against the pillow. My back arched and my breasts rose as my body recognized feelings of lust mixed with pleasure. I swallowed hard again as Brad drove his tongue deeper inside me, my legs twitching with every pass he made across Delores. I tugged his hair, tight in my fingers, with each moan and gasp he caused to escape me.

God, this feels good, ran through my mind on repeat. No longer caring about my lack of maintenance, I spread my legs further, granting Brad full access. And with full access, Brad's face disappeared like a lion eating a gazelle. And don't get me wrong, as much as I liked what he was doing, it wasn't the thing that was going to *get-me-off,* if you will. Never has been, *soooo* ... I did what I always do ... "Oh! Oh, God!" I moaned, gauging my vocals against the song now playing, U2's "All I Want Is You," keeping my voice a decimal lower. "*Braaaad!*" I wailed, hoping to really send my performance home. *And scene,* I smiled to myself as Brad eased. Unfortunately, it was only long enough for his tongue to refocus while his fingers caressed my opening below. *Damnit!* Not wanting to prolong this part any longer, I pushed myself away from him. "I just want you inside me." I said apologetically, not looking for sympathy.

"And we'll get there, I promise. But will you give me this?" Brad asked, eyes sparkling down at me.

I kindly acquiesced his request, saying nothing, I laid back down. And as our eyes met, his index and middle fingers disappeared in his mouth. Fingers wet; Brad slowly pushed them inside me. Having had nothing inside me for countless months, his fingers filled me, giving me a preview of what was hopefully to come.

Removing his fingers, I watched as he sucked me from them before sliding them inside me once again. My body welcomed the invasion as his tongue continued working its magic above them. I willed my body again to relax as my mind wandered, imagining *him* and what it would be like when *he* was finally inside me. Just the thought caused my body to begin climaxing. *Well, THIS was unexpected!* And even if *this* was something I was expecting, I wasn't ready for it! I had finally relaxed and now it was about to be over! *Who knows when this will happen again,* I reasoned as my body struggled against the inevitable. My lungs filled and then deflated rapidly as I panted into the air. I anchored my feet up to the edge of the bed in an attempt to push myself away from his mouth, but Brad's grip around my thigh held me firm as his mouth pushed against me, devouring me rhythmically while his fingers continued working themselves inside me. I gripped the bedsheet in one hand, his head in the other, "Oh, God!" I moaned, but this time was for real. My body convulsed as ecstasy poured from me and Brad drank like he'd found the fountain of youth. After what seemed like forever, but was not nearly long enough, every nerve in my body filled with deliriousness.

"You gotta stop." I laughed quietly, rolling my body toward his and urging him away from what was now too sensitive for touch. Wrapping my arms around his neck, I directed his face to mine. "Thank you," I whispered sincerely as another laugh escaped me. I was beyond happy because I had just orgasmed from someone other than myself, and orally, and it felt amazing. I let go of his neck, taking his gorgeous face in my hands. "Thank you," I repeated, intent on conveying just how grateful I was. Brad said nothing, but his smirk and look of satisfaction were enough. "All I Want Is You" became audible again as Brad brought his drenched lips to mine. Mouths connected, tongues twisted together, turning me on even more than before.

All of this was pure heaven to me. I love kissing a man after he has gone down on me, getting to taste myself from his tongue and his lips. And even more heavenly was feeling him, hard against my thigh. Brad pressed himself against me, down there, where I remained wet from his tongue and orgasm. I bit my bottom lip, imagining the very thing that was pressing against me and what it would be like once he was inside. I steadied my feet at the edge of the bed once again and eased myself toward the opposite side, now making room for us.

With more room made, Brad sat up, taking his lips that I could have kissed forever with him, and using his index finger, gave me the "just-a-second" signal. Scooting off the bed, he collected the safety gear Ava had so graciously provided. As much as I don't love condoms, I love STDs even less. And as reliable as my period-regulating IUD probably was, better to be safe than sorry. I wedged the pillow again under my head so I could watch as Brad removed the condom from its wrapper. He easily rolled it on, and I marveled at how a shiny condom can make a man look even larger than when it's … not wrapped.

Knowing he was safe, my body opened to him, imploring his return. Brad smiled as he descended over me, his weight on his elbow. His free hand gently removed the pillow from behind my head. Someone in his past must have disliked the pillow under her head during sex, as did I. Lost in his thoughtfulness, Brad's eyes locked with mine again, my connection with him was magical, and I felt my heart pound quickly against my chest.

Reaching down between us, Brad guided *what was so very hard,* to where I so desperately desired it. He brushed against me, lubricating himself before entering, and then he pushed.

My eyes rolled closed, and I pushed my head against the bed, forcing my back to arch. "Are you okay?" he asked softly.

I opened my eyes and beamed dreamily at him. "More than okay."

Reassured, Brad eased himself deeper inside me. A breath escaped me as he gently pushed, filling me as I had imagined he would. His lips grazed against mine as he pulled out, teasing me, and as his tongue entered my mouth, he pushed himself inside me again. Our mouths seemed to devour each other, his saliva, warm and sweet, dripped into my mouth. I rotated my hips to the left and then to the right, teasing Delores against him as my body responded to his rhythm of filling me up before leaving me almost empty. My insides tightened as they worked to pull him in as deep as possible, fighting his exit. Brad broke my rhythm, rearranging his right leg over my left, he stacked our legs, to where our pelvic bones now mashed against one another. Still on his elbows, Brad hovered above me. I craved the touch of his chest against my own and tried in vain to pull him to me, to feel his heart beating against mine. But Brad resisted, relentlessly teasing me as his body hovered inches above me. I pushed the back of my head against the bed, breaking from his kiss, and arched my body toward his until, at long last, I felt my nipples brush against his chest. Just the feel of his skin caused my breath to accelerate. With every inhale, my breasts met his chest, and with every exhale my back released against the bed. Five breathes in Brad caved, releasing his weight on me, pinning me under him.

Feeling the weight of his body and the warmth of his skin against my own almost brought me to tears. It had been so long since I had felt this kind of affection. I wanted to stay in this place forever, under his weight, as he pulled and then pushed himself rhythmically inside me. I blinked away any tears that had beaded at the corners of my eyes and began to inventory his body. The hair on his legs was soft against mine that were freshly shaven. The heaviness of his body pressed down on me, transferring the light sweat that was breaking on his skin, to mine. My fingers caressed his arms, tracing the outline of the V in his triceps; his breath, warm and labored with passion.

Brad's rhythm escalated. He exerted himself, faster and harder, as he pushed me to the edge. "Ah! Brad! I'm going to come again!" I cried out through gritted teeth. I wrapped my arms around his back and pulled him tightly to me.

"Kiss me," I begged breathlessly. Brad granted my wish, pressing his lips hard against mine. Our mouths broke only as moans escaped us and then Brad thrust himself forcefully inside me. I grabbed the back of his head in my hand as my other hand gripped his ass. My fingernails dug into his flesh, pushing myself onto him as far as possible. My eyes squeezed tight as my body exploded with ecstasy, forcing breath, mixed with moans, into Brad's mouth.

"Oh God. Oh God!" Brad groaned, thrusting himself faster and harder, "God!!!" he groaned louder, pushing himself deep, twitching and pulsing as warmth filled the condom inside me. My arms, exhausted, held his body tight, and I wrapped my feet around his calves as our bodies became one. Brad remained firm, pressing himself against me as the last bits of my own orgasm left my body.

"Holy shit!" he whispered, kissing me, while trying to catch his breath. His arms were shaking as he held himself up. He gazed down at me with a look of satisfaction until moments later, exhaustion won out and Superman's arms gave in. And like I was holding Kryptonite, his body collapsed, becoming dead weight on top of me.

"I gotta catch my breath. Shit," he breathed heavily against my ear. I, too, was fighting to catch my breath, which, beneath his weight, proved challenging. But I wouldn't change a thing, not for all the coffee in Costa Rica … and I *love* coffee.

Our limbs were now slack with exhaustion and Brad and I rested in silence. My "Chill" playlist had reached its end and, as our breathing slowed, I heard the faint song of crickets from outside the window.

I ran my fingers along his back and felt a shiver wash across his body. "You good?" I asked after a few moments of tickling his back.

Brad lifted his head to face me, a loopy smile spreading across his lips. "I'm good."

Rolling off of me, Brad lay to my side, propping himself up on his elbow. *Ouch,* I thought, no longer feeling the heaviness of his body penetrating my soul. I forced a smile to hide the strange ache I was experiencing and looked at Brad, a welcome distraction. He looked absolutely debauched. His hair was a mess and his cheeks, as far as I could tell, were flushed. His eyes sparkled against the outside light as he looked at me. We smiled into a kiss, my neck straining to meet his lips. Our teeth clacked awkwardly, but neither of us seemed to care. Brad found a pillow and placed it under my head, allowing our kiss to deepen. I felt his heartbeat against the side of my chest as he trailed his hands up and down my stomach, his palm lightly gliding over my skin. My body stirred under his touch, betraying my exhaustion.

"If we stay like this, I'm gonna get hard again," Brad began, pressing himself against me, "and I really need to get this thing off." Standing up from the bed, his eyes dragged themselves lazily over my body and he let out a sigh that made me feel beautiful, sexy, and satisfied. He slipped the condom off, tying it at the end before walking into the attached bathroom. He yanked some toilet paper off the roll, hiding the evidence, before tossing it into the small trashcan next to the toilet. *Definitely wasn't raised in a barn*, I thought, smiling as I watched him, still in disbelief that he was here and throwing away a used condom. Brad found the fresh washcloth Ava had left for me on the side of the tub and ran it under warm water, wringing it out before bringing it to me.

My smile broadened at his sweet gesture, and I wiped myself clean. "Thank you," I said, returning it to his outstretched hand.

"Of course," he said, finishing the rest of the water that was waiting for him on top of the armoire … on a coaster. Speaking of water, I sat up and guzzled down the rest of mine, only to discover it was not nearly enough.

"Hey, Brad?" I whispered, interrupting him rinsing out the washcloth. "Would you mind handing me a towel? I'm gonna grab us some more water."

"More water would be great," he said. I turned off the now-silent speaker and as I did, everything became dark.

"Nice!" I laughed, pulling off the towel Brad had tossed on my head, enjoying his playfulness. I wrapped the towel around my body, securing it at the center of my breasts. I retrieved our glasses, then headed out in search of hydration.

When I returned, Brad was sitting on the bed. I handed him his glass and he drank all of it before I could even get mine to my mouth, "Okay, no swimming for you for at least ninety minutes!" I said, my eyes wide.

Brad grinned into his glass. "Man, I was thirsty."

"Do you want me to get you some more?" I asked, reaching for his glass.

"I'm good but thank you." I took his glass and blindly felt for the coaster on the armoire. "Here, I got it," he said, taking it back from me.

"Maybe I've shrunk," I shrugged sitting down on the bed. Brad easily placed his glass on the coaster and sat down next to me.

"Any chance you wanna go again?" he asked, nudging me teasingly.

"Again?" I asked, swatting his arm in surprise. There wasn't much strength behind the swat, but Brad jumped like there was.

"I'm kidding. Don't get me wrong, I would love to go again, but truth be told that was my first time in a long time." Brad paused a moment. "Not twenty-two months long, but it's been … a lot of time."

My mouth twisted into a side grin as I tried to stop myself from smiling at what was more than likely, not true. Not only was my twenty-two months of celibacy ridiculous but knowing men the way I think I know men, Brad's idea of "a lot of time" was more than likely three, maybe four … weeks. Just like my definition of six inches is equal to a man's eight, nine, or even ten.

I stood and kissed his "lot-of-time" lips. "I need the bathroom," I said. "I'll be right back." I walked into the bathroom, closed the door, and flipped on the fan … I hate when people can hear me pee. I lifted the towel and sat, multitasking as I drank the rest of my water. Done with both, I left my glass on the bathroom counter and wiped myself. It was awkward not having any panties to pull up and I found it amusing that I had left the towel on, only for me to now take it off and hang it on a hook inside of the bathroom door. Naked, I stood at the sink and as I washed my hands, I noticed my mascara had flaked under my eyes. *Well, aren't you attractive?* I asked myself rhetorically. *Ta da!* Opening the top vanity drawer, I found exactly what I was in search of: makeup wipes. I was beyond impressed at Ava's forward-thinking skills. With the little bit of makeup, I had been wearing now wiped away, I looked around for lotion but realized I didn't need it. Gawd, I heart humidity!

Exiting the bathroom, I turned off the light, but left the fan on … white noise. As my eyes adjusted to the dark, I found Brad already snuggled under the covers. He lifted them up for me, patting my side, and I climbed in next to him. The yumminess of his cologne now mixed with the sweet scent of his sweat made me miss the future him. Brad pulled me to him and, wrapping his arms around me, directed me to lay with him like spoons in a drawer. I was pleasantly surprised at how natural it felt, spooning him like something we'd done with each other every night since I could remember. I loved feeling his body, naked and soft against my back, my butt, my legs, our feet so tangled I wasn't sure whose were whose. His left arm created a pillow under my head, and the other one wrapped around my rib cage.

"Are you comfortable?" he asked sleepily.

"I am," I answered, turning my face toward his. Brad and I kissed each other good night, as if it were a kiss we had exchanged the night before, and the night before that. It didn't take long before his breathing grew labored, and the soft melody of sleep escaped from him. Unable to join him just yet, I welcomed the stillness of the dark as my mind replayed the post-game film. *How was it that I had gotten so lucky?* I wondered, thanking God for this fleeting gift: Being in this man's arms, if only for one night. I yawned, hoping it was a sign that sleep would invade, but it eluded me. I wasn't good at this part. Trusting a man with sex was one thing. Trusting him enough for me to fall asleep with him … that's a different story.

chapter 4

I walked into Ava's kitchen the next morning, greeted by the rich aromatic smell of coffee and Ava's ridiculous shit-eating grin. She really was trying not to laugh and was *not* doing a very good job of it.

"*Sooooo* …" she began in her laugh-as-she-talked style, "How did it go?"

"Oh my gosh, Ava," I stared at her, shaking my head in disbelief. "Where to begin, gah!" I scooped the mug she was holding toward me into both hands and held it up to my nose. Closing my eyes, I breathed in one of the best things about mornings. The sweet aroma permeated my being as I gathered my thoughts. "Okay," I began, taking my first sip of coffee, "…so much to tell!"

I followed Ava as she led me to her patio, impressed by how spacious it was. Large enough to hold a wicker couch, two matching chairs, and a rectangular coffee table. Strategically placed potted flowers gave this space a comfortable, homey vibe. I set my mug on the coffee table, plopped my body down on the couch, grabbed one of the many decorative pillows and hugged it against my chest as I spilled the juicy details. "Okay, great kisser. I mean … delicious. And the sex! Ava! The sex was *soooo* good." I tilted my head back, feeling giddy because I had had sex and was here in person with Ava to tell the tale.

"Oh, I bet it was good," she said. A coy smile graced her lips, "Thin walls, remember?" My face flushed into what probably looked like a third-degree burn. "Oh my God!" I said, covering my face with the pillow. "Please tell me you didn't hear us?" my question muffled.

"Relax, relax," she said. "I turned on my white noise machine after the first moan and was out. Anyway, continue."

"Oh Gawww-Duh! I am so sorry," I moaned, removing the pillow from my face. "And thank you for the condoms, by the way," I quipped as a shiver of discomfort shot through me.

"Well, I'm glad someone got to use them!" she belted out, relieving my discomfort, which forced a laugh out of me. Unfortunately, Ava was having a dry spell herself. She's not a one-night stand kind of girl, so it may be a while. I retrieved my coffee and took a sip, then lowered it, resting it on my chest.

"So …" I began, recalling my night with him, "… it was good. At least I think it was good." I said, trying to convince myself. "But here's the thing. As soon as we got to the bedroom and he unzipped my dress, all I could think about was how my nether regions probably looked like the Amazon jungle!" My face contorted like I had just eaten something disgusting. "I was half-tempted to give him a machete!" My description got Ava laughing, almost to the point of hysterics. I love how easy it is to make her laugh. She was clearly amused by my description and, to be honest, so was I. I smiled into my mug, taking another sip, I held it in my mouth, enjoying the taste before I swallowed.

"Ava," I said dryly, "I hate to admit it, but I've been a little lazy down there because, you know, waiting for the one and all. I mean, I figured by the time I met my dude and we decided to be intimate with each other, I'd have time to prepare shit down there!" I said, a little deflated. "Who knew Austin would bring out my inner slut?" I shook my head in a *no-no-no* motion as I ranted, "I mean, seriously?"

"Okay? *Soooo*?" Ava urged, motioning with her hands for me to get on with the details.

"So, I mean, yes, we did it. But I'm telling you," I paused to look at her. "I was so preoccupied. And he is so hot, and I feel so unruly down there, I don't think I was able to thoroughly enjoy myself. Okay, wait. I enjoyed myself, trust me, just maybe not as much as I would have had I been *ready*. Right?" I air quoted *ready,* exhaling loudly. "I can't believe I went twenty-two months with nothing and then I couldn't even fully enjoy it because I was so embarrassed by my gynascaping," I said, fake crying.

"Or the lack thereof?" Ava grinned. I lifted my head and as our eyes met, we began laughing to the point of tears as Ava continued making jokes about how getting past my Amazon jungle would be nothing compared to the cobwebs awaiting him in my gyna.

"Okay, two favors and then I'll tell you the best," I said calming down. I held up my index finger signaling my first favor, "Ibuprofen," I then added my middle finger, signaling the second favor, "and a bag with ice in it. My gyna bone has a heartbeat!"

"Okay, Booboo, ibuprofen and ice for the p-bone coming right up!" Ava stood from her chair and disappeared into her apartment. I placed my feet on the edge of the coffee table and laid my head back, staring at the beautiful cloudless blue sky. *What the heck, Lake?* I asked myself as memories of the previous night came drifting back.

"Here ya go, Boo. Little ice and some ibuprofen." Ava had returned, interrupting my thoughts. I swallowed the two pills she offered, then the full glass of ice water. I placed the ice pack gently on my pelvic bone and looked up at her with relief.

"Okay, okay, so tell me!" she said excitedly.

"Okay," I began, shaking my head, "I honestly can't believe everything that happened."

"So, are you okay? That you did... all... you know?" Ava asked. Her eyes, as big as they were, grew even bigger as she looked down at the ice pack covering my gyna.

I was completely at peace with the events of the night and answered, "I am more than okay. But," Ava's phone rang, interrupting me.

Ava looked at her screen and I could see her dilemma as to whether she should answer. "Ugh, crap. Okay, hold on, I gotta take this. It's Shirley." Hurriedly she answered, "Hi, Mom!" Covering the mouthpiece, she whispered, "Can I tell her?" Ava's eyes were all a-glitter while her eyebrows raised in a hubba-hubba motion.

"Duh, of course you can." I whispered back.

"So, Mom! We went out last night and Lake hooked up with a total hottie!" Ava couldn't say any of it with a straight face. She laughed the entire way through.

"She did?!" I could hear Shirley and her southern drawl like she was sitting right there with us. "Oh, Lake, how fun! Where did she do this hooking up? Ava! You didn't let her go home with him, did you?" She asked almost scolding her.

"No! Mom! God no!" Ava sounded insulted. "She brought him back here! Mom, I was admittedly a little skeerd, so I locked my bedroom door."

"You locked your bedroom door and left poor Lake out there all defenseless?"

"Yes, Shirley!" I shouted, "She locked me out!" I couldn't help but laugh as I realized, yet again, just how absurd the entire night was.

"It's all okay, Mom. She's alive, and so am I!" Ava said, lighting up a cigarette. Not being a smoker, I stood up to go inside. "Sorry," Ava whispered sincerely, waving the smoke away from my direction.

"No worries," I mouthed back, grabbing my coffee and ice pack. I closed the door behind me but could still hear Ava giving her mom the G-rated details from the previous night. Back in the kitchen, I poured myself another cup of coffee with creamer and watched as two tiny drops fell into my mug. *Please have more creamer, Ava,* I prayed silently, opening the refrigerator door. "Yes!" There in front of me was another bottle of French vanilla creamer. "That's my girl!" I praised, pouring a good amount into my coffee. I like my coffee the same color as peanut butter. Taking a sip to be sure my ratio was correct I sang out, *"Peeeeerfect!"* then tucked the ice pack into the waistband of my pajama shorts.

Holding the mug with both hands, I walked down the hall to the guest room. Once inside, I placed my mug where my water had sat the night before. I laid down on the bed that had so recently seen a *lot* of action and reminisced about the night before. Unsure of the time, I glanced at the clock. It was only 8:00 a.m. and already it was seventy-five degrees outside. I was exhausted from lack of sleep, and as the cold air from the air conditioner breezed over my body from the vents above, I finally relaxed.

"Sorry about that!" Ava, having finished her cigarette and phone call with her mom, walked into the room. Suspiciously, she eyed the bed. "Is it safe for me to sit here?" she asked, now looking like she was the one who had just eaten something disgusting. I relieved her wariness, informing her that we did *almost* everything under the duvet. Cautiously she sat down, making yuck faces all the way. Lying on her side next to me, she propped herself up on her elbow, her big brown eyes searching mine intently. "K, spill."

I stared up at the ceiling, scanning my memory as I tried to recall where I had left off. "So, being with him really was good, as in great. And we did it so many times I swear I may have quite possibly fractured my pelvic bone." I looked down at the ice pack resting carefully on my PB. Playfully, I continued, "He had dinner at the Y, and then he gave me the hot beef injection … a couple times actually, once as soon as we got here, as you heard." I shuddered again. "And then he woke me up a couple hours later."

"Gggrrooosss. Lake! Hot beef injection?" she asked laughing through disgust.

"Okay, he put his peni-erecti in my vag-i. Is that better?"

"Maybe, just a little," she said, her voice and face contorting into sophistication. "How'd you two leave it? Are you going to see him again?"

"I don't know." I shrugged, "He gave me his number, but ... I don't know. And if I don't call him, it's for no other reason than there would be no reason, right? He lives here and I don't." I gave her a resolved smile/not smile. "You're not going to believe what happened," I paused, changing the subject. I pursed my lips again and side grinned.

"What? Did the jungle freak him out?" Ava asked, a little too seriously.

"I'd say something freaked him out. Not sure it was the jungle but thank *you* for bringing *that* back up!"

"I'm sorry, Boo. Continue."

"So, we did it, like I said, but the second time he definitely lasted longer so we did it, every way imaginable." Ava looked horrified. "Okay, ya dirty bird, we didn't do it *that* way! According to Relationship 101... that's the boyfriend hole. Duh."

"*Gggrroooossss*! But, okay, good, I mean, you do you, but ... not in the... *you know*!"

I couldn't help but laugh and roll my eyes at Ava, thinking I'd let a guy I just met in the "BFH."

"Would you like me to continue?" I asked, sounding like a kinder-garten teacher who was about to take recess away from an unruly class.

"Yes, Booboo, I'm sorry."

"Okay, *eh-em* ... so, this morning, he rolls over and gets on top of me and is ready to go again. Ava, I came so many times," I said, disbeliev-ing it myself. "And he came," I held up my index finger, then my middle finger and finally my ring finger, "three times."

"Oh, I like those odds!" Ava said encouragingly at first, "But," she looked puzzled, and then looked to be doing calculations in her head, "I only gave you two condoms."

"Yeah. So, he climbs on top of me this morning and he's already hard. I was like; *I am so sorry Brad, I can't.* And I really couldn't. I was so sore. So, he starts kissing me, which was good, no morning breath at all and as we're kissing, he moves from on top of me to the side of me, so now I'm lying next to him, right?" I looked at Ava to make sure she was following.

"Okay, yeah," she answered with curious assurance.

"And he takes my hand to his... wiener... sorry, I mean his peni-erecti and I start, you know, jackin' him off." As I said this, Ava belted out a huge uncontrolled laugh.

No longer able to look at her as I continued, I looked back to the ceiling. "And then," I paused as I gathered my courage. Taking a deep breath, I turned to face her, "he came." Pausing again for dramatic effect, I waited for Ava's laughter to die down before delivering to her, "And shot his jizz in his eye." My eyes widened and my lips pursed together as I tried to stop from smiling the *holy-shit-what-the-fuck* smile that was begging to escape.

Ava's laughter ceased abruptly. "Wait. What?" she said, looking at me blankly. I stared at her a moment and then said it again. Slowly this time.

"He... shot... his... jizz... in... his... eye. As in, his jizz went from his wiener to his eye." My index finger demonstrated the wiener to eye, jizz movement. "I kid you not." I concluded.

Ava stared at me, unmoving, like she was paralyzed until, like watching a light bulb receive electricity, it hit her. "Oh, my gosh!" she yelled. Rolling onto her back, Ava started to belly laugh but then stopped as abruptly as she started. She looked at me again, like she was waiting to see if I was joking, seeing I wasn't, she started laughing again. "Oh, God! What did, what did he do?" she asked between coughing, crying, and howling fits.

"He freaked! I mean? Ava! I could tell he was, you know, *coming* and then he sat straight up like a college kid who'd slept through his finals alarm and was like; *Shit, shit, it's in my eye.* And I was like; *What's in your eye?* And of course, I would ask that because, *who the fuck* jacks so far, *on the third go round*, that it shoots into his own eye?"

"Oh. My. Gosh! What did he do?" Ava prodded, trying to catch her breath.

"He went into the bathroom and started to flush his eye with cold water, like it was lighter fluid that had shot in there!" Ava had yet to stop laughing.

"And what did you do?" she implored, her eyes searching my face for what could possibly come next.

"I got him a washcloth and was like, *I'm not even sure why I got this for you. Just trying to be helpful.* Then I put my hand on his back and was all: *Or do you need me to go out and get you the morning-after pill?*"

Ava, now crying, hacking and coughing, rolled to the side of the bed, fell off, stood up, and walked out of the room. A minute later she was back with a glass of water and her inhaler. "Oh God! You have got to be kidding me!!" She continued, like the last few minutes had never passed.

"I wish I were! At least that made him laugh and kind of lightened the mood. Honestly, he was a champ about it, but I think we were both a little traumatized." I shook my head, covering my face with my hands. "I mean! Who does this shit happen to Ava?" I asked rhetorically, throwing my hands in the air in a *what-the-fuck* manner before answering myself, "Me, obviously! That's the fuck who!"

"Oh Lake!" Ava laugh-talked; her voice raspy. "I mean? Where do you even go from there?"

"Well … you call him a cab and send him home! Thank God there was a cab close by."

* * *

Shortly after the jizz-in-the-eye incident, I walked with Brad, hand in hand, to the main road. Our fingers interlaced, my stomach flip-flopped, and my heart felt weird, knowing this would be the last time I'd feel his hand holding mine.

As we reached the curb, I glanced down at my chest, irritated to see I was nipping out. How on earth a person could nip through a white cotton cami in this wrinkle-removing, skin-plumping humidity, was beyond me. But with facing handsome Brad, and my sensitivity to his touch, apparently nothing was safe. I hugged my arms around my body in a futile attempt to hide them.

"Despite everything that happened this morning," Brad pulled my hands back to his, interlacing our fingers as we faced each other, "I had a great time, and I'd love to see you again." He said, gripping my fingers tighter, "Are you cool with me giving you, my number?" My heart leapt; excited, scared, and hesitant at his asking. Even though I was unsure, I retrieved my phone from the pocket of my light pink pajama shorts.

"Sure, and by the way," I said, handing him my phone as I tried to conceal the joy I felt, at having his phone number, "I'm really trying to act like none of that just happened in there, but your eye keeps reminding me it did."

"Is it still red?" he asked, handing me my phone back.

"Beet red my friend." I said just as a yellow cab pulled up. "Hey Brad?" I began, a little more seriously.

"Yes, Lake?" he mimicked, his tone teasing me lightheartedly. His mimic caught me off guard and I smiled. But my smile faded as quickly as it had appeared, knowing what I was about to say.

"I don't think you'll hear from me," I winced, "and it has nothing to do with what happened this morning." I looked up at him, holding my hand to my forehead to shade my eyes from the rising morning sun. "Geographically speaking, I just don't know that it would be a good idea."

Brad stepped off the curb and opened the door to the cab, asking the driver if he would give us a second. Getting the okay, he turned back to me, taking my hands in his once again. "I think I understand." Brad pulled me close to him, embracing me, and my body sank into his for what was more than likely the last time. Kissing the top of my head, Brad broke our embrace before moving back a step so he could look at me, "You have my number. I would love to hear from you." Face to face we stood there, me on the curb and him on the street as he looked at me for what was probably only a few seconds but seemed much longer. I could tell he wanted to say something but decided against it. Contemplating whatever it was, he lightly tapped the side of his fist on the top of the cab and then kissed me swiftly one last time.

"I hope you call," is the last thing his throaty baritone voice said to me.

He didn't look at me again but got into the cab and closed the door.

Standing in the quiet, warm Austin morning, I watched as Brad's cab pulled away, driving off into what I am guessing for Brad was a jizzy-eyed sunrise. *Too soon?* I asked myself. Overly impressed at my cleverness, I spun around toward Ava's apartment. Freshly fucked and happy, I sang, "Oh my jizzy-eyed surprise, sundown to sunrise, we gonna dance all night to this DJ," I paused and flipped my phone open, continuing the tune, "and those are all the words I know, yes those are all the words I know." I stopped singing, clearly unable to continue as I did not know any words past the chorus. Phone open, I searched "Brad." Interestingly enough, he was the only "Brad" in my phone. *Brad Weems.* I stared down at his name and held my breath as I pushed the edit button. Tapping the down arrow, I scrolled until I saw: *Delete Contact.* Blowing the air out of my lungs, I hesitated again as the *Delete Contact* or *Cancel* options appeared on my digital screen.

You know this is for the best, Lake, the voice of reason urged. But as I stood there on the black-paved drive, the flowering bushes that lined the sides of the entrance distracted me. *God, it's beautiful here.* I closed my eyes and basked in the warmth of the now-November sunrise, wrestling with my new dilemma. When I opened my eyes, I looked down at my index finger poised over the button that would delete Brad from my life. But then hope crept in, like she always does, and my heart pleaded ... *What if?* I moved my finger to *Cancel*, pushed it, and then quickly checked to make sure it was cancelled before smacking my phone shut. Decision made, for now anyway. With that, butterflies filled my soul as I thought back to the amazing night Brad and I had shared and my hope of *what if.* And as my mind went to places that were ridiculous, a chuckle escaped me, grateful that the one thing I had in common with Cameron Diaz was her smile and not her hair gel.

acknowledgments

To my *friends* who listened to countless stories over the years, telling me I should write a book, your laughter and encouragement brought this on. You have only yourselves to blame.

To DK, in the beginning you were there. Meeting with me, trading hair services for your time and energy, reading through my rough (and I mean rough) drafts, making sense of them and encouraging me to continue. To Doc and Matil, thank you for listening to my ideas (there have been a few over the years, eh?) for your encouragement and your laughter. Thank you for feeding me, not judging my life (or the amount of food I can put away) and for being the big brother and sister I never had but wanted and needed desperately. I wouldn't be the person I am today had it not been for your commitment to my desire for growth.

To LF, thank you for allowing me to visit you in AZ, providing a beautiful place in the sun to write. Thank you for your time and for being a great sounding board as well as helping me with editing. To LG, girl you took on a huge task, reading chapters, suggesting changes (delicately), and giving me insight, all while plying me with delicious home-made cocktails on your beautiful flower filled patio. The time and energy you put into this book has been exhausting. It wouldn't be what it is today if it wasn't for your dedication and talent.

To my boys, though this is a book you know you will never read, you continually encouraged me to finish it, excited for me, because I was excited for it.

And to the rest of you... too many to mention. You, who knew about this endeavor and encouraged me with your questions, ideas, and excitement.

Much love and appreciation to all of you!

about the author

lake/not lake, resides in Colorado but is always planning her next beach vacation and or open water ocean swim. If she could, she'd live in the ocean, only going to the surface for air. Her greatest joy is spending time with her grandkids, marveling at the way they think, how easily they laugh, and how much they love.

lake/not lake, loves swimming, writing, journaling, hiking, meditation, spending time with family and friends as well as time alone. Her plan is to continue to write…even if no one wants her to. ;)